Jesus Lives With Us

Carolyn Byers

4

REVIEW AND HERALD® PUBLISHING ASSOCIATION
WASHINGTON, DC 20039-0555
HAGERSTOWN, MD 21740

This author assumes full responsibility for the accuracy of all facts and quotations as cited in this book.

This book was
Edited by Penny Estes Wheeler
Art direction by Linda Anderson McDonald and Stephen Hall
Cover art and illustrations by Chris Molan
Cover design by Stephen Hall
Type set: Palatino 12 pt.

PRINTED IN U.S.A.

Library of Congress Cataloging in Publication Data

Byers, Carolyn.
   Forever stories / Carolyn Byers.
     p.   cm.
   Summary: Retells in story fashion the life of Jesus from the age of twelve to His death.
   1. Bible stories, English—N.T. Gospels.   [1. Bible stories—N.T.]   I. Title.
BS2401.B74   1989
232.9—dc20   89-37757
                                                                            CIP
                                                                             AC

     ISBN 0-8280-0504-4

Dedication
for
Brenda, Branton, Brady,
and Brani

Contents

In the Temple

"Our feet shall stand within thy gates, O Jerusalem . . ."

The boy kicked a round pebble as He sang. He was on His way to the Passover services in Jerusalem.

He raced ahead of the donkeys and wagons. He bumped the same little stone with His sandal and sang on.

"Peace be within thy walls, and prosperity within thy palaces." *

It felt good to be alive on that spring day. Wildflowers laced the path's edge. An eagle soared overhead. Sparrows twittered in the bushes.

Jesus had looked forward to this day for years. Mary and Joseph had told Him about the Passover service. "When You are 12 years old, we will take You to the Temple. When You are 12, You not only will be a Son of Abraham; You will be a Son of God."

Now Jesus was 12 years old. He gave the stone one more little kick.

_____
* Psalm 122:2, 7

A large group of people walked from Nazareth to Jerusalem. The trip took days. Friends visited along the way. Few people knew that God's Son walked with them.

When Jesus was born, several people welcomed His birth. Bethlehem shepherds came to see Him. Wise Men brought Him gifts from a faraway country. Two old people in the Temple asked to hold Baby Jesus. They thanked God

for letting them see Him. Now that Jesus was older, though, no one seemed to notice Him.

Mary knew that Jesus was God's Promised One. Joseph knew it, too. But they didn't discuss it often. Once in a while, Mary talked to Jesus about it. But only when they were alone. Mary wasn't sure that Jesus knew who He was.

Jesus slowed down to ask Mary a question. "Will Simeon and Anna be at Jerusalem this year?" Simeon and Anna were the old people that held Jesus in the Temple when He was a baby.

"I doubt it. They were very old when You were born."

For a long time Jesus walked along in silence. He was thinking of the stories Mary had told Him about His birth.

"Look ahead. There's Jerusalem, Jesus."
Joseph shaded his eyes. Jesus squinted in the
sun. Far away He could see trees and
buildings.

"Where is the Temple?"

"It is that big white building on the hill."
Joseph tugged on the donkey's reins. Someone
in the group broke into singing again. "Our
feet shall stand within thy gates, O Jerusalem
. . ." Another joined. And another. Jesus sang
too. Across the valley, He could hear others
singing.

Once inside the city, Jesus helped unload the
donkey. He brought back some water for Mary.

"Jesus," Joseph said, "we need to go buy a lamb for the Passover service."

"Where do we get one?"

"They sell them near the Temple gate."

Jesus followed Joseph. They wove their way through the crowds. The closer they came to the Temple, the more carefully they moved. They didn't want to step on anyone's foot or trip over things for sale.

Jesus watched as Joseph chose a lamb. He picked out a pure white one. Joseph fumbled in his clothes for his money.

"Baa, baa," the lamb bleated.

"Jesus, You carry the lamb." Joseph lifted it to Jesus' shoulders.

Joseph paid the merchant. Then father and Son walked through the Temple doors. They went across the open courtyard and up some steps. They stood under a wide gateway, waiting for a priest to help them. Finally a priest motioned for them to come.

Jesus held out the lamb to the priest. The priest took it. Jesus and Joseph knelt as the priest prayed. "Father, forgive us for our sins. Thank You for Your lamb whose blood saves us. Send our King soon. Amen." The priest had said the same words all day long. His voice sounded like·a squeaky wagon wheel.

The priest lifted his knife to kill the lamb. It hurt Jesus to watch.

"Next!" The priest motioned to another family.

Joseph saw Jesus wipe His eyes. "It reminds us of the time they painted the doorposts in Egypt," Joseph said. "The blood saved the oldest boys from death."

During the next few days Jesus spent little time with His parents. Mary didn't worry, for Jesus always chose to do what was right. Jesus spent His time in the Temple, watching the priests. As Jesus watched, God spoke to His heart.

Suddenly Jesus knew what the lamb stood for. "I am God's lamb," He said softly.

Five, six, seven, eight days passed. It was time to go home. Mary and Joseph loaded the donkey. They chatted with old friends as they walked toward Nazareth. They didn't see Jesus, but they didn't worry. They thought He was with the other children.

When the group stopped to camp, Mary asked, "Where is Jesus?"

"I don't know," Joseph said. "I'll go look for Him."

"Do you know where Jesus is?" he asked a little boy.

"No. I haven't seen Him."

"Where's Jesus?" He asked it again and again. But nobody knew.

"He must be back in Jerusalem," Joseph told Mary.

Mary gasped. "What shall we do?"

"We cannot go back in the darkness," Joseph said. He put his arm around Mary. "We will have to wait until morning."

The next morning they hurried back to Jerusalem. They headed for the Temple, crossed the courtyard and climbed the steps. Finally, in one of the hallways, they heard Jesus' voice. He was talking to the priests.

"You say the Redeemer will be king over Israel. What does Isaiah mean when he talks about the lamb?" Jesus' voice was gentle. But He clearly wanted to know.

The priests looked puzzled.

"What do *You* think?" The room was quiet.

"Jesus. Jesus," Joseph called to Him.

Jesus turned and walked to them.

"Son, why did You treat us like this? We were worried about You." Mary's voice scolded Him.

Jesus looked puzzled. He pointed a finger upward. "Why did you search for Me? Didn't you know that I would be in My Father's house?"

Mary bowed her head. Tears sprang to her eyes. *Now my Son understands*, she thought. *He knows He is the Son of God.*

God's Son

Psh, psh, psh, psh. Jesus held the board with one hand. He sawed with the other. *Psh, psh, psh, psh.* One end of the board fell to the floor. With the eye of a craftsman, He could see the cut was right.

Jesus was growing older. He worked with his father in the carpenter shop. He liked working with wood, but He knew he would not work in the shop forever.

It wasn't until He was almost 30 years old that the change came. A customer came into the carpenter shop.

"There's a new preacher by the Jordan River. I think his name is John. He is telling people to get ready for the Lord to come. Hundreds of people are going out to hear him. He tells them to quit being mean and selfish. When people give their lives to God, John baptizes them."

Jesus gave the man a long look. He knew He must leave home soon.

A few days later Jesus hung up His saw. He put away the drill for the last time.

"Mother, I must go now." He gave her a long hug. "Goodbye."

Mary bit her lip and blinked back tears. She felt both joy and sadness. She watched Jesus walk away. Where the road turned, He stopped and waved to her.

When Jesus reached the Jordan River, He listened to John preach.

"God loves you," John said. "He wants to care for you. But He cannot unless you change and obey Him."

"How do we do that?" asked a man in the crowd.

"Turn from your selfish ways. Give clothes to the poor people. Share food with people who are hungry," John replied.

Then he asked, "Do you want to be God's children?"

"We do," several shouted.

"Do you want to obey God?"

"Yes. Yes."

"Then come and be baptized."

Jesus heard John call. He walked forward. John saw Him coming. He studied Jesus' face. He had never seen a face so kind and loving. Instantly John *knew*. He knew this was Jesus Christ. This was the One he'd been preaching about. This was the day he had waited for. Jesus stepped into the water. "Please baptize me," He said.

John bowed his head. "I need *You* to baptize me," he replied quietly.

"No, John, I must be baptized by you. It is the right thing to do," Jesus told him.

John obeyed. Together John and Jesus waded into deeper water. John prayed. Then he gently dipped Jesus under the water. Jesus made His way back up the riverbank. There He knelt and prayed.

As Jesus knelt on the wet ground, bright beams of light encircled Him. A lovely dovelike form hovered over His head. A voice spoke from the sky. "This is my beloved Son, in whom I am well pleased."

John heard the voice. "Behold the Lamb of God!" he cried.

The words rang in Jesus' ears. *My beloved Son, My beloved Son, Behold the Lamb of God, My beloved Son.*

Jesus' mind whirled. He must get away and think. *What was He, the Son of God, supposed to do now?*

Jesus started down a road, away from the crowds. On and on He walked. The road became a sandy path. The sandy path narrowed into a trail made by rabbits and foxes.

As Jesus walked, He prayed. "How can I make people know that God is good?" He asked. "How can I fight with Satan? How can I do it?"

By a scrub bush, Jesus stopped. He knelt on the hard ground and prayed. The sun slid behind the hills. The stars

came out. Night passed. The sun rose and kissed Jesus'
head. It climbed higher. The day grew hot. Still
Jesus prayed.

God heard His Son's prayer. Just as He hears the prayers
of all His children. God helped Jesus understand what His
work would be.

"You must heal the sick. Comfort sad people. Tell
children stories. Not everyone will like You. Some will hate
You so much that they will kill You. But love them anyway.
Then people will know what God is like. Then they will
know how much God loves them."

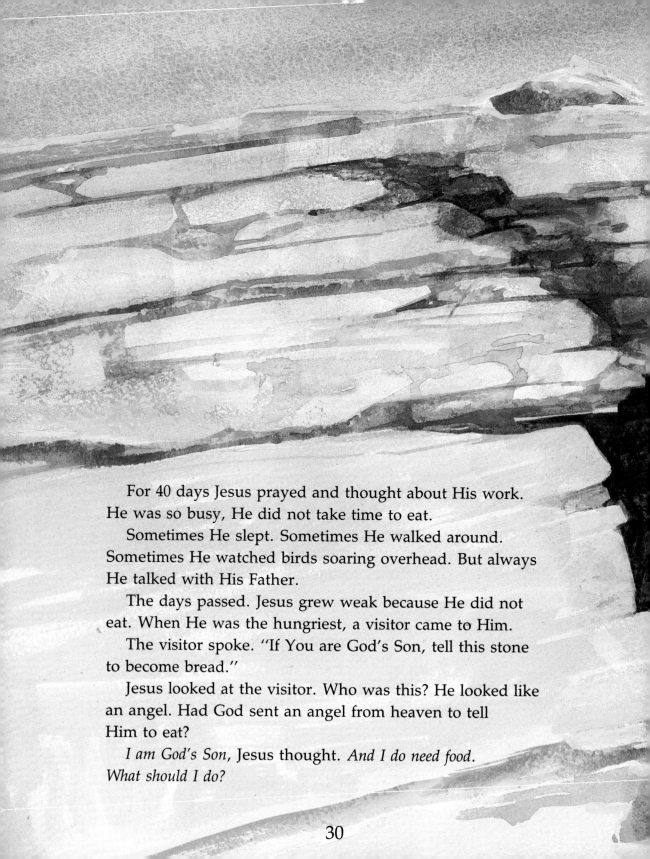

For 40 days Jesus prayed and thought about His work. He was so busy, He did not take time to eat.

Sometimes He slept. Sometimes He walked around. Sometimes He watched birds soaring overhead. But always He talked with His Father.

The days passed. Jesus grew weak because He did not eat. When He was the hungriest, a visitor came to Him.

The visitor spoke. "If You are God's Son, tell this stone to become bread."

Jesus looked at the visitor. Who was this? He looked like an angel. Had God sent an angel from heaven to tell Him to eat?

I am God's Son, Jesus thought. *And I do need food. What should I do?*

His mind kept working. *If I am God's Son, I can tell the rocks to be bread. And they will be bread. But wait. Is this what God wants Me to do?*

Jesus' stomach ached. His head ached. His thoughts traveled on. *This visitor says if I am God's Son. I am God's Son. This is Satan! I choose not to obey him. I do not want Satan to care for Me, no matter how hungry I am.*

Jesus looked the visitor in the eye. "The Bible says that man does not live by bread alone. He also lives by the words of God!" *

* See Matthew 4:4

Satan saw that Jesus would not make bread. So he decided to tempt Him in another way. Satan carried Jesus to the top of the Temple in Jerusalem. God let Satan do this so that the good angels would see what Satan was like.

"If You are God's Son, then jump!" Satan ordered. "The Bible says that angels will take care of You."

Jesus' thoughts raced. *If that is what the Bible says, maybe I should do it. I can show Satan that I am God's Son. But wait. What does the rest of the Bible say? No, God doesn't want Me to be foolish. God doesn't want Me to try and hurt myself. I won't jump.*

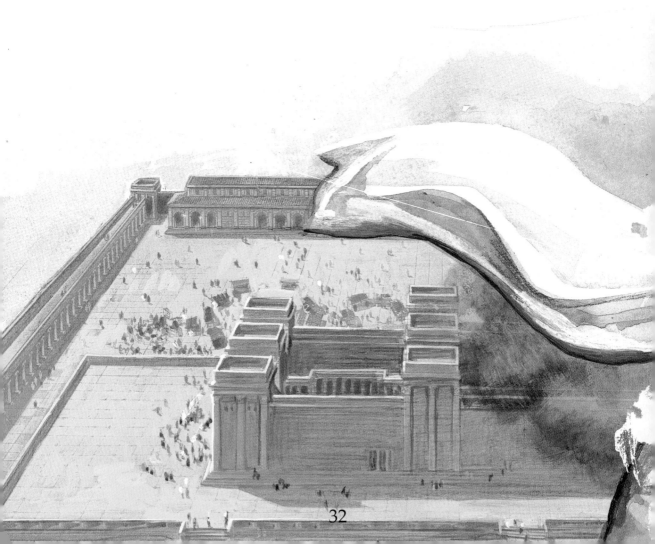

Jesus looked Satan in the eye. "The Bible says, 'You shall not test the Lord.' " *

Once more Satan tried to get Jesus to obey him. This time he took Jesus to a mountaintop. Jesus could see rolling hills and templed towns.

"You can be king over all this land. All You must do is worship me," Satan said. He tried to smile and look friendly.

It sounded easy to Jesus. Much easier than trying to help people who would someday kill Him. But wait. Was this what God wanted?

* See Matthew 4:7

"Get behind Me, Satan!" Jesus commanded. "The Bible says, "You must worship the Lord your God. Serve only Him." *

Jesus knew He was God's Son.

When Jesus said God's name, Satan ran away.

Jesus fell to the ground, ready to die. It had been hard work fighting with Satan. He was very weak. He had not eaten for 40 days.

---

* See Matthew 4:10

God had been watching all the while. And the good angels had been watching. The angels waited for a signal from God.

"Go!" God told them. "Take food to Jesus and give Him a message."

The angels hurried to give Jesus food. As He ate, the angels talked. "Your Father loves You," they said. "You fought well."

One Day With Jesus

"Behold the Lamb of God."

Jesus had been in the desert praying for 40 days. All that time, John waited for Jesus to come back. Now he was happy to see Him again. John told his followers that Jesus was the Lamb of God.

A man named Andrew nudged Peter, his brother. "We must go with this Man."

"We'd better hurry then. He is walking away."

Quietly the two followed Jesus. Jesus turned and asked, "What are you looking for?"

"Teacher, where are You staying?"

"Come and see," Jesus invited.

From that day on, Andrew and Peter went everywhere with Jesus. Ten more men joined them. The 12 men were called Jesus' disciples.

In a seaside city one morning someone shouted, "Jesus is coming in a boat."

Everyone who heard the news told someone else. Housewives left their dirty dishes and baking to go see Jesus. Fathers closed up their shops. Children raced around asking questions. "Will I get to see Him heal somebody? Will He come to our house? Mommy, are we ready to go yet? Hurry! I want to see Jesus."

By the time the disciples tied up the boat, a crowd had gathered. Jesus talked to the people. He healed their sick. He stayed with them all day long.

Then Matthew, one of His disciples, invited Jesus to come to a big dinner at his house. Many of his friends from the tax office would be there.

Jesus greeted Matthew's friends. He enjoyed the lovely food fixed for Him. While He was still eating, though, someone tapped Him on the shoulder. Jesus looked around.

"My little girl is dying" a man cried. "Please come put Your hands on her so she will live." His eyes were red and watery.

"I'll come." It didn't matter where Jesus was. If someone asked for help, Jesus went. Jairus, the girl's father, held the door open for Jesus.

Jesus found many people waiting for Him outside Matthew's house. He inched along behind Jairus. "Bless my baby," a mother begged. She held the baby out for Jesus to touch. He patted the baby's bald head.

"Please heal my friend. His head hurts," another said. Jesus touched the fevered forehead. The man smiled.

Jesus saw a lady with tears in her eyes. "God loves you," He said. Her eyes shone. She wiped away her tears.

Jairus tried to hold the people back so Jesus could move faster. But suddenly Jesus stopped.

"Who touched Me?" He asked.

The people looked startled. Who touched Jesus? Hundreds of people touched Him! That was a strange question.

"Who touched Me?" Jesus asked a certain lady.

She started crying. "I did. I only touched a corner of Your robe, though." She put her hands over her face and wept. "I have been sick for 12 years. I went to many doctors, but they could not help me." She looked up with a shy smile. "But when I touched Your robe, I was made well."

Jesus returned her smile. "You are well because you chose to trust. Go in peace."

"Jairus, Jairus." A man pushed through the crowd. "Sir, your daughter has died," he said sadly. "There is no need to trouble the Teacher."

Jesus overheard the words. He searched Jairus' face. "Don't worry. Just trust Me. Your daughter will be made well."

Jairus nodded.

It wasn't long until they could hear the wail of flutes and loud crying. Already the family had hired mourners. The noise bothered Jesus. When He reached those dressed in sackcloth, He stopped. "Shhh," He said. "Why do you cry? The little girl is not dead. She is sleeping."

The mourners' tears turned to laughter. One snorted, "He doesn't think we know a dead person when we see one."

Jesus followed Jairus into the house. "Tell them to go outside," Jesus said.

Jairus motioned for the mourners to leave. The little girl's mother came into the room with Jairus and Jesus. Three disciples followed. Jesus saw that the little girl was not breathing. Her skin was pale. Her eyes were closed. Her hands were cold.

Jesus went to her bed. "Talitha, I say to you, get up!"

Instantly she wiggled. Her eyes opened wide. She smiled and looked quizzically at Jesus. She looked at her parents and at Jesus' three disciples.

"Who are they?" she asked her father.

"This is Jesus," he said. "Jesus made you well. And these are some of His disciples."

46

Her mother sat down beside her. She stroked her daughter's long hair. Happy tears chased down her face.

"Jesus. This is Jesus," the little girl whispered.

Jesus looked at her with a happy smile. Then He turned to her mother. "She is hungry after being sick. Go get her something to eat."

Jesus was the only one who remembered that she had not eaten for several days. Her mother hurried off to the kitchen.

When Jesus left Jairus with his happy family, He still had work to do. Before Jesus slept that night, He healed two blind men. He also cast a demon out of a man who could not talk.

At meal time that night dozens of families discussed Jesus.

"Did you see that blind man jumping around?"

"Yes. If I were him, I'd jump too. Now he can get a job and buy food for his family. His wife is already planning a banquet to celebrate."

"I'm happy for Jairus. He loves his little girl. What if Jesus hadn't come today?"

"I don't know. I've never seen anything like this before. Never before."

Thirty Silver Coins

Twelve disciples trailed Jesus. The tall one was Judas. He carried the money. If Jesus bought food, Judas paid the merchant. If a poor family needed food, Judas bought it. Once in a while Judas took money for himself.

This Sabbath afternoon Judas went to Simon's house. Simon opened the door. Judas followed Jesus in and bowed to Simon.

"I'm happy to be here. It is gracious of you to invite us."

"It is my privilege," Simon replied. "This is my chance to thank Jesus for healing me of leprosy."

51

"It will be nice when Jesus is king in Jerusalem, won't it?" Judas stood as tall as possible. He didn't say all that he thought. He didn't want Simon to know that he planned to become very important when Jesus was king.

Judas looked about the room. The table was spread with mountains of delicious food. Martha was setting more bowls of food on the table. A man named Lazarus stood nearby. Jesus had raised him from the dead. Martha's sister, Mary, stood by Jesus. She seemed to always tag after Jesus.

"Come, enjoy the meal." Simon showed them to their couches. Martha scurried about, serving food.

When the meal was half done, Judas sniffed the air. Instantly he recognized the scent.

It was spikenard—the perfume that rich people used! Judas searched the room with his eyes. Who could afford *that!* Then he saw Mary pouring it on Jesus' feet. So *she* did it. She must have used all her money to buy it.

"Such a waste," Judas grumbled. "Why didn't she give me her money? It would buy many meals for the poor." Judas spoke loudly. He wanted Mary to hear him.

Mary's face turned red. She tried to hide. She hurried to rub off the perfume with her long hair.

Jesus heard the unkind words. "She has done a beautiful thing." Jesus spoke so everyone could hear. "She honored Me before I die."

Judas pushed back his plate. *I've had enough,* he thought. *Jesus is not good to me. He is always talking about dying. I'll change things. Just watch. I'll show who is the smart one.*

Judas' thoughts boiled as he walked toward the Temple. *I'll make Jesus fight, I will. He will win. Then He will be king and I will be important.*

At the Temple Judas bowed before the high priest. Other priests sat around the room. Judas guessed they were trying to think of a good way to get rid of Jesus. After all, the people liked Jesus better than they liked the priests.

"Sir, I hear you want to catch Jesus." All eyes turned to Judas. None answered. They were surprised. This man was one of Jesus' disciples!

"I think I can help you—that is, if you can come up with a little money."

"Well, well. How much money?"

"I'll give you a bargain. I'll help you for the price of a slave."

"It's a deal. Thirty silver coins."

Judas bowed again. "I'll get back with you later." Then he turned and strode away. He felt good. He would force Jesus to be king.

Sunday, Monday, Tuesday, and Wednesday Judas brewed his secret plan. *We'll get a crowd together to catch Jesus*, he thought. *Jesus will knock them down and get away. Then we'll make Him king. I will be honored and very important.*

On Thursday Jesus asked the disciples to buy a lamb. It was Passover time. They would use the lamb for the Passover meal. Judas paid for the lamb.

At the Passover supper, Jesus washed each disciple's feet. He washed Andrew's feet. He washed Peter's feet. He washed Matthew's feet. In the same way He washed Judas' feet, too. Judas felt disgusted. Only slaves washed dirty feet! *If Jesus doesn't act like a king,* Judas thought, *He deserves to die!*

Judas kept making his plans. *I'm going to lead the priests to the garden where Jesus prays. Nighttime is best. Then Mary and her friends won't bother us.*

Jesus interrupted his thoughts. "This grape juice is like My blood. Every time you drink it, think of Me." Judas took the drink that Jesus passed. He didn't want to look different.

"And this is like My body." Jesus held up a piece of broken bread.

"One of you is going to sell Me to the enemy," Jesus said. Judas looked up. *How does He know? Who told Him?*

The disciples looked horrified. Who would do *that?* "Is it I?" Peter asked. "Is it I?" asked Andrew. "Is it I?" all the disciples asked. Only Judas was left. They all looked at him. But Judas saw only Jesus' eyes. They were full of love. What should he do?

"Is it I?" Judas stammered.

"It is."

Jesus' words gave Judas one last chance to choose. Did he want to follow the One who loved him? Or did he love money and power more?

Judas stood up. His feet turned toward the Temple.

That night Judas came to the garden where Jesus prayed. Soldiers, priests, and ruffians chased behind. Some carried clubs. Others had long knives.

"What do you want?" Jesus asked.

"Jesus of Nazareth."

"I am He. If you are looking for Me, let these people go their way." Jesus pointed to His 11 disciples.

Judas came up and kissed Jesus. That was his signal to the soldiers to catch Him.

A soldier tied Jesus' hands behind Him. Another dragged Him away. Judas waited for Jesus to escape. Judas knew Jesus could kill them all if He wanted to. But He didn't.

Judas followed the crowd to the courtroom. Judas waited and watched. *When is He going to show who He is?* he wondered. He saw the soldiers whip Jesus. He saw them put an old king's robe on Him. He saw them press a thorny crown on His head. He saw a man spit in Jesus' face. Judas waited.

The crowd of people in the courtroom grew larger. Someone yelled, "Crucify Him." The mob took up the chant. "Crucify Him! Crucify Him!"

Judas watched. Jesus didn't say anything. He didn't even look angry. He was quiet, as quiet as a lamb.

"Crucify Him! Crucify Him!"

Judas could stand it no longer. *He's not going to fight. He's not going to make Himself king. He's going to die. I sold Jesus to die!*

Judas felt his money bag. The 30 coins jingled.

"Crucify Him! Crucify Him!" the crowd chanted.

They can't crucify Jesus. He isn't guilty. He didn't do anything wrong. Judas ran forward. "Jesus is innocent!" he cried.

Judas grabbed the money bag and threw it down. The coins jangled as they hit the stone floor. The crowd quieted.

Then Judas knelt before Jesus. "You are the Son of God. Save Yourself."

Jesus looked at Judas with kindness in His eyes. "This is why I came into the world."

Judas turned and went out into the night.

The men in the courtroom saw that Jesus had done nothing wrong. But He was condemned to die.

Jesus walked up the road to Mount Calvary. On the way He passed a tree. Poor Judas. He had hung himself from the tree. It brought tears to Jesus' eyes.

At the top of a little hill, soldiers nailed Jesus' hands and feet to a cross.

Jesus hated the wickedness of those around Him. He longed for quiet and peace. He could have run away. But He didn't. God could have saved Him. But God didn't. Jesus died so that everyone everywhere could see what Satan is really like. And what God is really like.

That afternoon Jesus died so that people could choose to follow Him. And be saved.